Disclaimer

The publisher and the author make no warranties or representations with respect to the completeness or accuracy of the contents of this work and specifically disclaim all warranties, including without limitation warranties of fitness for a particular purpose.

No warranty may be created or extended by sales or promotional materials.

The advice and strategies contained herein may not be suitable for every situation. This work is sold with the understanding that the publisher is not engaged in rendering legal, accounting, or other professional services. If professional assistance is required, the services of a competent professional person should be sought.

53

interesting things to do in your
lectures

Revised and updated by Anthony Haynes and Karen Haynes

P&H

ISBN: 978-1-907076-22-0 (ePub edition)
978-1-907076-23-7 (PDF edition)
978-1-907076-24-4 (Kindle edition)
978-1-907076-30-5 (paperback edition)

Published under The Professional and Higher Partnership imprint by The Professional and Higher Partnership
Registered office: Mill House, 21 High Street, Wicken, Ely, Cambs, CB7 5XR, UK

Company website: www.professionalandhigher.com

This edition published 2012.

Based on an earlier edition by Sue Habeshaw, Graham Gibbs, and Trevor Habeshaw, published by Technical and Educational Services Ltd (first published 1984). Revised and updated for this edition by Anthony Haynes and Karen Haynes.

© The Professional and Higher Partnership Ltd

This publication is in copyright. Subject to statutory exception and to the provisions of relevant licensing agreements, no reproduction of any part may take place without the written permission of The Professional and Higher Partnership Ltd.

Credits
Text development and abstract: Anthony Haynes
Copy-editing: Karen Haynes
Cover design: Benn Linfield (bennlinfield.com)
Cover image: Rika Newcombe (www.rikanewcombe.co.uk)
Text design and typesetting: The Running Head Limited (www.therunninghead.com)
E-book conversion: ePub Direct (www.ePubDirect.com)
Printer: Printondemand-worldwide (www.printondemand-worldwide.com)

Contents

Abstract	ix
Professional and Higher Education: series information	x
Publishers' foreword	xi
Preface to the first edition	xiii
Glossary	xv

Chapter 1	**Structuring the process**	**1**
1	Briefing	3
2	Flagging	7
3	Ground rules	9
4	Students' questions	11
5	Orientation	13

Chapter 2	**Improving students' notes**	**15**
6	Swop	17
7	Memory	19
8	Virtual lectures	23
9	'Now write this down'	25
10	Displaying your notes	27
11	Review	29
12	Looking at students' notes	33

Chapter 3	**Using handouts**	**35**
13	Theme summary	37
14	Model your discipline	39
15	Problems	41
16	Questions	43
17	Uncompleted handouts	45
18	Article	47
19	Reading guide	49

Chapter 4 Structuring and summarising content — 51
20 Structuring — 53
21 Objectives — 55
22 Advance organiser — 57
23 Displaying the structure — 59
24 Progressive structuring — 61
25 Repetition — 63
26 Simultaneous messages — 65
27 The three most important things… — 67

Chapter 5 Linking lectures — 69
28 Last week, next week — 71
29 Preparation activities, follow-up activities — 73
30 Spot the links — 77
31 Theme lectures — 79
32 References — 81

Chapter 6 Holding attention — 83
33 Mini-lecture — 85
34 Breaks — 89
35 'Now look at me when I'm talking' — 91
36 Ottoman railways — 93

Chapter 7 Active learning during lectures — 95
37 Lecture tutorials — 97
38 Buzz groups — 101
39 Problem centred and syndicate groups — 103
40 Pyramids — 105
41 Tiers — 109
42 Reading — 111
43 Quiet time — 113
44 Drama — 115
45 Students as teachers — 117
46 Using the audience — 119
47 Debate — 121

Chapter 8 Checking on learning   **123**
48 The instant questionnaire   125
49 The three most important things ... for students   129
50 Start with a test   131
51 Finish with a test   133
52 Spot test   135
53 'Are there any questions?'   137

Abstract

53 practical ideas for developing lectures are presented. They cover: structuring the lecturing process; improving students' notes; using handouts; structuring and summarising content; linking lectures to each other; holding the students' attention; active learning during lectures; and monitoring learning. For each of the ideas, a problem or issue is identified and a practical teaching or learning method is proposed. Overall, the ideas are designed to help reflective practitioners in professional and higher education broaden their repertoire of pedagogical techniques.

Key terms: higher education; learning; lectures; pedagogy; post-compulsory education; professional education; study; teaching.

Professional and Higher Education: series information

Titles in the Professional and Higher Education series include:

53 interesting things to do in your lectures
53 interesting things to do in your seminars and tutorials
53 interesting ways of helping your students to study

Publishers' foreword

The original edition of *53 interesting things to do in your lectures* was published in a series called 'Interesting ways to teach'. It was written by Sue Habeshaw, Graham Gibbs and Trevor Habeshaw – all of them experienced teachers – and published by their company, Technical and Educational Services. The book proved popular amongst peers in post-compulsory education and ran to several editions.

Now that the original authors have retired from teaching, we are very pleased to have acquired from them the rights to this and other titles from that series. Much of the original material remains fresh and helpful. We have, however, revised and updated the text where appropriate. In four places (items 10, 14, 30 and 36), the original text has been replaced wholesale.

Anthony Haynes & Karen Haynes
The Professional and Higher Partnership Ltd

Preface to the first edition

This book contains 53 suggestions for things to try out to make your lectures more interesting and effective. While there are sound theoretical justifications for these suggestions (and occasionally even empirical evidence in their support) they are offered here simply as ideas worth trying for yourself.

The suggestions are grouped under broader headings for convenience and are cross-referenced where this is helpful. Every suggestion in this book has been tried out, and seen to work, by the authors. Each one carries its own number, and a brief description of the problem or issue it addressses and a description of the method.

The book is not meant to be read from start to finish, but rather to be dipped into as each suggestion should make sense on its own. Where appropriate we have made reference to original sources of ideas or to places where fuller explanations can be found.

While the book has been written primarily with teachers in further and higher education in mind, the ideas it contains can easily be modified and adapted for use by teachers in secondary schools, schools or nursing, and management training, by instructors on government training projects and others.

Graham Gibbs
Sue Habeshaw
Trevor Habeshaw

Glossary

Conventional lecture
50–55 minutes of largely uninterrupted discourse from a teacher with no discussion between students and no student activity other than listening and note-taking.

Seminar
A session during which prepared papers are presented to the class by one or more students.

Tutorial
A discussion session, usually dealing with unspecific content, or a recent lecture or practical. Chaired by the teacher, it may have any number of students from one to 20, or so.

Class
Any session during which students are gathered together in the presence of the teacher.

Chapter 1

Structuring the process

1 Briefing   3
2 Flagging   7
3 Ground rules   9
4 Students' questions   11
5 Orientation   13

1 Briefing

Lectures are used by teachers for an extraordinary variety of purposes. Their relationship to other course elements such as reading, tutorials, assignments and practicals differs markedly from one course to another. What it is sensible for students to do during such different lectures also varies enormously. However, students may respond as if a lecture is a lecture is a lecture, and behave identically in entirely different situations which demand quite different learning activities. To brief students at the start of a lecture is to tell them what sort of a lecture it is to be, and what sort of learning activity it might be sensible to undertake. Briefing students not only influences their behaviour so that they make more appropriate and effective use of your lecture in their learning, but also has an impact on their perceptiveness and discrimination as learners. They will begin to recognise that different learning tasks make different demands and start extending their repertoire of learning responses accordingly.

We offer a variety of different briefings here to illustrate what we mean:

a   'The reason I am lecturing in the way I am is that I want you to see some live examples of the applications of legal principles to specific cases. I'm expecting you to learn the principles from your text books, and to learn to apply legal principles by tackling the legal problems I've prepared for you which we will discuss in tutorials. In this lecture what I want you to pay attention to is the way I go about tackling such problems. I want you to be able to do it like me. There is only any point in noting down the details of the cases if this helps you to understand and remember the legal arguments involved. OK?'

b   'Your text book deals with these calculations of forces in rigid structures perfectly adequately, but you may find it difficult to follow on your own. I'm going to use each of these lectures to go over one chapter: to explain the methods and notations the text book uses, and to highlight particular problems or interesting bits. You could probably manage without these lectures. You certainly can't manage without going through your text book very thoroughly. I'm lecturing to make your work through your text book that much quicker and easier. You should make notes *in your textbook* as I go along, rather than take full notes.'

c   'You are only going to get a grip on the social psychology of groups by reading, and reading quite widely. I've given you a substantial reading list; read as much as you can but you will find the reading hard going. The authors I've chosen all use different language and make different assumptions even when considering the same phenomenon. The theoretical perspectives from which writers approach topics are very varied and greatly colour the way they write. So the purpose of my lectures is to try to stop you from getting lost when you start reading. I'll familiarise you with the terminology and highlight some landmarks along the way. I want you to consider my lectures as maps to a strange land. Take the sort of notes you'll find helpful to have next to you when you're reading.'

d   'This lecture introduces you to dialectical materialism. It's a difficult concept and one that underpins much of what the remainder of the course is concerned with. Now I could just give you a neat definition to write down or some quotes from Engels for you to copy. But that wouldn't help you much. Instead I'd like to talk around this concept and just try to explain it as best I can; I want you just to try and understand it. Don't bother taking any notes; just listen and think. I'll be

1 *Briefing*

asking you to discuss some aspects of dialectical materialism later in the lecture.'

Briefing is concerned with the overall function of the lecture and is therefore distinct from **Flagging** (see 2) which is used to draw attention to the nature of specific actions you might take within a lecture.

2 Flagging

Flagging is explaining what you are doing, and why. Teachers often introduce an activity or the next stage of a session without flagging it, assuming either that students already know what it is they are supposed to do and what they are supposed to get out of it, or that students don't need to know: all they have to do is follow instructions. But people's ability to undertake tasks depends crucially on their understanding of the task – and not just their understanding of what the task is, but of why it is a sensible or useful thing to do. Many of the suggestions in this book may need thorough flagging the first few times they are used or students may feel hesitant and reluctant to engage in the suggested activity.

For example, you might want to introduce a break into your lecture – something you haven't tried before – and say, 'OK, stand up, stretch your arms and give a big yawn'. This is likely to be met with embarrassed giggles and not much movement. To flag this would be to explain, 'You've been sitting still in this gloomy, stuffy room for 40 minutes now. It may help you to be comfortable and to stay alert for the next 20 minutes if you use the next minute to move around a bit. Stand up, stretch your arms, have a good yawn, try anything you like to release the physical tension and relax your muscles. I'm going to do the same'.

If you wanted to introduce a buzz group exercise (see **38 Buzz groups**) you might say, 'Now, in pairs, I want you to look at the map on the next slide and decide what Christaller's theory would have to say about the location of the towns'. For students unused to such activity during a lecture, and unused to working with one other student, and certainly unsure whether this was some sort of trick test, this might be a difficult task to get going on. To flag it might involve explaining, 'It's important that you are able to apply Christaller's theory to specific places and I need to know whether you are able to do this before I continue. So I'm going to set you a very brief task to do. It might be difficult to get going on your own so work together with your neighbour'.

It is probably better to be over-explicit in your flagging than to assume your audience already knows why you are doing what you are doing.

3 Ground rules

All lectures have ground rules though these are not normally explicit. Unless you have informed your students of the specific ground rules you want to operate they will probably assume that conventional ground rules are operating. These conventional ground rules may include:

a   The responsibility for the success of the lecture is entirely the teacher's, who will do all the preparation, all the real work during the lecture, and make all the decisions during the lecture about its content and process.

b   The lecture topic will relate directly to the syllabus and to likely exam questions on it.

c   The student's role is to sit quietly and listen: interrupting is undesirable and talking with a neighbour is absolutely banned.

d   The teacher will lecture uninterrupted for 55 minutes.

e   No work, other than listening and taking notes, is required of the student.

f   Attending lectures is a solitary, unco-operative, even competitive, activity: students work for themselves.

g   If the teacher wants to know if students are attending, bored, interested, comprehending, or whatever, she will have to ask a specific student: such information is not to be offered spontaneously (which would offend the teacher) or in response to general questions addressed to the whole class (which would offend students suspecting creeping).

h   Only geeks sit at the front.

You may feel that these ground rules are not those you would like to operate. In this case you may need to take some time at the start of the course, or of specific lectures, to make your own preferred ground rules explicit.

You could say, 'On this course the lecture periods will be rather different from what you are used to. In them I expect students to tell me if they think I'm going too fast, if they need a break, and so on. So if you feel you just can't listen any more and your writing hand is aching, it is perfectly OK to ask me to stop for two minutes to catch up and rest. I'll *expect* such suggestions from you'.

Students' assumptions about ground rules may be soundly based in their experience of many conventional lectures. You will need to be very explicit about your own ground rules, refer to them repeatedly, and behave appropriately (e.g. by accepting a student's request for a break, in the example above) for students to start operating according to your ground rules. More radical changes in ground rules (e.g. concerning sharing of responsibility for preparation, or concerning the acceptability of direct comments about the quality of your lecturing) may need to be introduced gradually. Some other suggestions in this book (see **4 Students' questions** and **35 Now look at me when I'm talking**) concern the operation of specific ground rules.

4 Students' questions

Students are often confused because some teachers allow them to ask questions during the lecture, some allot time for questions at the end and some only accept individual questions when the rest of the students are packing up and leaving. They are particularly confused because teachers don't usually explain what their practice is when they first meet the students. Students who are not given any indication to the contrary will tend to assume that they can never ask questions in lectures.

It is very helpful to students if you not only make it clear what your attitude to questions is but if you also support this statement with appropriate behaviour. That is, if you say that it's all right for them to interrupt the lecture, don't look annoyed when they do; if you say you'll take questions at the end, allow time for them; if you say you'll answer individual questions, give those individuals your full attention when they approach you.

This is a specific form of **Ground rules** (see 3).

See also **'Are there any questions?'** (53).

5 Orientation

Some teachers rush into lecture rooms and start speaking immediately, only to find that they feel disorientated, the students aren't ready and they need time to set up presentation media. It is worth pausing before you start your lecture and giving yourself time to orientate yourself by looking round the room, rehearsing silently the names of some of the students, chatting briefly with those at the front, cleaning the whiteboard, checking your audiovisuals, or arranging your notes.

It's also helpful if the introduction to your lecture is such that students don't need to start writing straight away but have their own orientation period at the start whose function is to remind them what it's like to be in one of your lectures as well as to introduce the lecture and link it with the previous week's work.

You can even begin to orientate your students before the lecture starts by displaying a slide of the total lecture programme or the structure of that day's lecture or by playing a CD or DVD which will provide a context for your lecture: baroque music for a lecture on baroque, for example, or a scene from the appropriate play for a drama lecture.

If you explain the principle of orientation to students and they see the point of it, they will learn to orientate themselves without your help. They can do this before the lecture by looking through their notes or reviewing the previous week's work with a friend.

If you decide to introduce quiet time into your lectures, you can make the connection and point out to your students that one of the purposes of quiet time is that of reorientation (see **43 Quiet time**).

Chapter 2

Improving students' notes

6	Swop	17
7	Memory	19
8	Virtual lectures	23
9	'Now write this down'	25
10	Displaying your notes	27
11	Review	29
12	Looking at students' notes	33

6 Swop

Note-taking can make heavy demands on students' attention and leave them little opportunity to think about what is being explained. Also students' notes are seldom comprehensive and completely accurate. Both these problems can be ameliorated by students sharing the task of note-taking in some way.

At the end of a lecture, or after each major section, students can simply swop their notes with their neighbour and read through them to see if major points have been covered, factual details recorded correctly, and so on. It may take only a couple of minutes for students to undertake such a check and then correct their own notes.

To help attention, students in pairs can do deals with each other to take turns in note-taking. One has the responsibility to take full notes while the other is free to attend to what is being said and to think about it. After a section of the lecture is complete, or half way through, or after alternate lectures, these roles can be reversed. At the end the notes are exchanged to create a full set. In this way students are free to attend to at least half the lecture material.

7 Memory

One problem with note-taking in lectures is identified by the cynical description of lectures as methods of transferring information from the notes of the teacher to the notes of the students without passing through the heads of either. It is perfectly possible to take verbatim notes without thinking about them, or even being aware of what they might be about, as any audio typist will tell you. While note-taking in this way may increase the likelihood of producing an accurate set of notes for subsequent reference, it does not do much for learning. And subsequent reference may not be of much use if there was too little thinking going on to make sense of what was being recorded. The basic dilemma is that to a certain extent the aims of understanding what is being said, and recording what is being said, are incompatible goals. The more likely you are to achieve one goal, the less likely you are to achieve the other.

One way around this dilemma is to separate the two goals and achieve them in sequence rather than attempt to achieve them in parallel: by only allowing note-taking to take place from memory after a section of the lecture is complete. To illustrate how this might work we will describe an agricultural engineer we have observed teaching. He forbad note-taking while he was talking in order to gain the students' attention and used visuals to illustrate what he was explaining (the way a seed drill worked). After about 15 minutes of such explanation he stopped, displayed the diagrams he had built up and explained so far, and said, 'Now I'd like you to take notes on what I've explained so far. Draw diagrams, list points, do whatever you want to record the key points and any details you think you'll need later on. You can have as long as you need. You'll have a chance to check whether you have forgotten anything or got anything wrong before I go on to the next thing'. After the 5–10 minutes the students needed, he then used a method for allowing students to check and improve their notes (see **6 Swop**).

In practice this results in:

a   far higher attention during explanations as students know they will have to remember and write notes in a few minutes. Attention is devoted to listening and thinking rather than being split between thinking and note-taking;

b   more questioning from students who, instead of copying down what they don't understand, need to make sense of the explanations if they are to remember them and take notes from memory;

c   smoother and faster explanations which do not have to keep being held up to allow the last point to be copied down verbatim by the slowest note-taker in the group;

d   notes which are brief and which only pick out the main points in a form which makes sense to the student rather than extensive copied notes which do not discriminate between key points and trivia, and which are structured in the teacher's way;

e   a learning check. Looking at students' notes taken in the conventional way can tell you whether students have perceived the important points, but can't tell you whether they have learned them;

f   learning during the lecture. Students are not always conscientious or effective in learning from their notes after the lecture;

g   improving the students' listening and comprehension skills.

Asking for notes to be taken from memory is likely to shock and alarm students the first time and they may initially be very bad at it (which in itself says something about the level of learning which takes place in conventional lectures). The introduction of this method requires proper explanation (see **2 Flagging**) and an adequate opportunity for students to check that they have remembered and noted down the important points. Time consuming note-taking, such as the drawing of complex diagrams and tables, can be avoided by the use of handouts (see especially **17 Uncompleted handouts**).

8 Virtual lectures

Webcasting of lectures has many benefits, both for off- and on-campus students. Sometimes the latter will miss your lecture for good reasons. Some students will attend your lecture but only partially understand it, or find it difficult to take notes from, or find it fascinating and want to check some facts or references for accuracy. A video (or audio) recording can solve all these problems.

Year by year you probably change your course around, dropping some topics and adding others. But the topics you discard are unlikely to have become entirely irrelevant or out of date. It is more likely that in your latest way of seeing and presenting things the old topics are simply of less interest or fit in less neatly. Last year's lectures on topics you have now dropped would very likely be of interest and use to students in the same way that last year's text book is still useful even though a new edition has been published. It can be useful to offer these discarded lectures even when no timetabled slot remains. You may be worried that your credibility will crumble if students hear that last year you said something different from this year. But the reality is that knowledge is not so very fixed, and contrasting interpretations and revisions of explanations are good for student's developing sense of relativism.

For all these situations a recording will be more comprehensible and useful to students if it is linked with a handout which provides an outline structure of the lecture. This can of course be the same as the handout provided for those who attended the original lecture or provided in a course guide.

Pausing and rewinding a recorded lecture enables students to gain a better understanding of the lecture material and potentially make better notes. However, these buttons also introduce the temptation to spend ages making an almost verbatim transcript. Students may need reminding that trying to write down every word the lecturer says is not good note-taking practice. Providing a linked handout with the key points of the lecture can help reduce this problem. Such handouts could also include a reminder link to recommended resources on effective note taking.

9 'Now write this down'

Inexperienced students, especially those new to a subject, can have a good deal of difficulty deciding what to note down and what to leave out. Common strategies are to write as fast as possible with the doomed intention of recording everything, and haphazard selection, noting what is easy to note: facts, dates, verbatim catch-phrases, etc. No amount of advice about structuring notes, using key words, and being intelligently selective, is at all helpful in such circumstances. These students can't perceive the structure and don't know what the key points are, and so have no basis on which to be selective.

For such students it can be helpful deliberately to highlight the crucial points, and guarantee that at least they are recorded fully and accurately, by highly selective dictation (or instructions to copy from a slide).

Explaining why you want something written down can be helpful if only to alert students to future occasions when they might recognise the need themselves (see **2 Flagging**). A handout with selected quotes would save the time of having to dictate. 'Now write this down' might be used as a halfway house to more demanding methods (such as **7 Memory**) and is probably inappropriate for more sophisticated students except for very specific uses.

10 Displaying your notes

It can be useful to students to make a sample of your lecture notes available to them – for example, on your department's virtual learning environment. 'Notes' here means just that – a preparatory, perhaps sketchy, document rather than text that has been polished in any way. The advantages of displaying your own notes include the following:

a   They may well be more sparse than the students' own and so demonstrate how a subject can be encapsulated concisely.

b   If, when you revise or update your notes, you use the 'track changes' function on your word-processing package, this will help to demonstrate to students that knowledge is not as fixed or monumental as it may seem.

c   Your notes may well be highly structured with strong emphasis on the most important ideas. Students listening to an extended lecture often miss elements of the structure or fail to grasp the relative importance of ideas. Seeing your notes will encourage them to try to see the wood for the trees.

11 Review

Students often have to go straight from your lecture into someone else's, or into a practical session, or a tutorial, or at least embark on some other different and demanding activity immediately after your lecture has finished. They seldom have an early opportunity to review your lecture by working on their notes or by undertaking a task requiring use of the content of your lecture. Even if they do have the opportunity they may not have the inclination to do so in the context of the social pressure to have a coffee and a chat.

Yet review is one of the most powerful and easily demonstrated devices for improving learning from lectures. And the sooner after the end of the lecture the review takes place the greater is its effect – the best time being immediately afterwards. Despite the crucial role of review in learning, and the reality that it seldom takes place after lectures, it is still common for teachers to lecture right up to the last minute, and even to introduce new information and ideas at the end.

Review can be built into the lecture plan as an activity taking place in the last few minutes of the lecture. We are referring here to a review undertaken by the students and not a summary undertaken by the teacher (see **27 The three most important things**). Such summaries would normally precede the students' review. Such reviews can take various forms. We offer two examples:

a (46 minutes into a 50-minute lecture)
'OK, now I'd like you to go back through your notes quietly on your own. Read through them. Remind yourself of the ideas we have considered. Make sure you understand what you have written down. Add things if it helps to make them clearer. Mark in a coloured pen anything which doesn't make

sense, or where you know you have missed information or suspect you've got it wrong. You have three minutes.'

(During this time you could circulate, quietly picking up individual queries.)

'Now your three minutes are up. I'd now like you to draw a line across the bottom of your notes and under that line write down what further work you need to do on the topic of this lecture before you would feel you have got on top of it. You may have specific queries you want to raise in the tutorial: note these down. You may need to check with someone else's notes that you haven't missed something out. You may feel you need to work through some examples before you feel confident: note this down. You may want to read something specific from one of the references I gave you: make a note of exactly what you want to read about, and where you will find what you want to read about. You have one minute.'

'OK, that's the end of the session.'

b (50 minutes into a 60-minute lecture)

'OK, so we have dealt with four types of sedimentation in this lecture. Here they are on the slide. I'd like you to turn to your neighbour so as to form pairs. One of you take types 1 and 3 and the other take types 2 and 4. In turn explain these four types to each other. Be brief, and just summarise the main features. You have two minutes for each explanation. I'll let you know when two minutes are up and it's time to switch around and go on to the next type of sedimentation. Now here's the tricky bit: you must give your explanation from memory! You must not refer to your notes or ask the other person. Off you go.'

(During the eight minutes you call out, 'OK, two minutes are up. Swop around and start the explanation of the next type of sedimentation. Do this now even if you haven't finished the last one. Off you go'. You may need to cruise around to check that students are following instructions, and to give some help to those who are stuck.)

'OK, you have tried to give these explanations from memory. Now check through your notes to see what you got right, what was missed out and so on. You have two minutes.'

'Now you ought to have a pretty clear idea what you know and understand and what you don't, and whether your notes are any use, so you also ought to have a clear impression of what follow-up work there is still to do on this topic before you can explain all four types from memory – because that is the sort of thing you will have to do in the exam. That is the end of the session.'

Your students may be quite unused to the notion that they should actually be expected to know anything or explain anything at the end of a lecture. The first time you ask them to they may baulk and be confused. The first example here is much less demanding and threatening than the second. The second can be very powerful in:

a   influencing the way students pay attention and take notes during the lecture;

b   highlighting inadequacies in notes which the kind of review in the first example might not reveal;

c   highlighting the need for specific follow-up work for the students.

The activity of having to explain is a much more effective review than that of simply reading through notes. Reading is such an essentially passive review as to leave students with a vague feeling of familiarity with the subject and a false sense of security about what has been learned.

It is possible to lead up gradually to the method illustrated in the second example by allowing students a couple of minutes in which to prepare their explanations, using their notes. This has the advantage of allowing students to check the adequacy of their notes without putting too great an emphasis on memory or risking severe embarrassment when explanation proves to be beyond them.

Such challenging methods may need clear flagging, and may initially warrant prior notice, e.g. 'At the end of this lecture you will be asked to explain to your neighbour two of the four sedimentation types which we are going to look at. So be prepared and pay attention!'

Quiet Time (see **43**) may be used by students for reviewing material, but unlike the examples offered here, quiet time is under the control of students to use as they wish.

12 Looking at students' notes

Many of the difficulties experienced by students in taking notes in lectures are caused by the teacher. Some styles of lecture are just difficult to take good notes from. They can be too fast, too abstract, too unstructured, too complex in structure, have their structure insufficiently signposted and their main points insufficiently highlighted, or just be too long and boring to attend to. However even excellent presentations can cause problems for note-taking when inappropriate assumptions are made as to the level of students' sophistication as learners. An effective way to improve the quality of students' notes is to improve your lecturing. But knowing what aspects of your lecturing are problematic for note-taking may not be easy. The sea of scribbling students you are faced with may not give you too many clues as to what they are finding difficult to note.

One way of gaining this valuable information is simply to borrow a couple of students' notes for an hour or so after the lecture and have a good look at them. If students are reluctant to part with their own set of notes for fear of losing them you could offer to make a photocopy after the lecture. Students may try very hard to write 'good' notes if they know in advance that their notes are to be scrutinised but this merely makes it more likely that any deficiencies in them are caused by your lecturing rather than by the students' indolence or lack of attention. Useful information can be gleaned from the amount students write in their notes, how this quantity is distributed between the different sections of the lecture, whether the structure of the lecture is reproduced, whether key points are omitted, whether excessive factual detail predominates rather over thoughtful statements in the students' own words, and so on. Problems identified in this way may be tackled either directly through other ways of improving notes (see **6–11**) or by introducing new lecture methods (see especially

20–27) or by reducing the need for note-taking by using student handouts (see 13–19).

The use of students' notes to identify problems in what has been learned could equally well be categorised as one of the methods of obtaining feedback on lectures (see 48–53).

Chapter 3

Using handouts

13 Theme summary 37
14 Model your discipline 39
15 Problems 41
16 Questions 43
17 Uncompleted handouts 45
18 Article 47
19 Reading guide 49

13 Theme summary

Perhaps the most difficult aspects of courses for students to perceive and learn about are the higher-order conceptual frameworks which structure the subject matter and the course itself. Often abstract and built upon a thorough understanding of the separate components of the subject (as presented in separate lectures) these overall themes can pose real problems for students especially in their note-taking. For example in a history course on 'Contemporary Perspectives on Medieval Europe' it may be alternative analyses of social change which form these higher order frameworks, and the underlying themes in any particular week's lectures. Methodological issues and aspects of the philosophical basis of the subject discipline itself often form such themes.

Handouts which summarise such themes, and which point out those aspects of the particular lecture which bear on these themes, may be particularly useful to students, especially those new to the subject or to note-taking.

14 Model your discipline

Lectures commonly seek to do two things at once – to convey knowledge and to introduce students to a discipline. The latter may be difficult to achieve – students may not recognise it as an aim and there may not be a common vocabulary for discussing it. As a result, it is easy to leave learning about the discipline – as opposed to acquiring knowledge within it – implicit.

You can use the layout of your handouts to display the cognitive structure of your discipline. For example, try summarising your lecture on one side of paper, divided into four boxes. In the first box, list the key items of knowledge – the **concepts** or **pieces of information** – covered by the lecture. In the second, list the **skills, methods** and **techniques** that you demonstrated or referred to in the lecture (for example, controlled experiment, correlation, or textual analysis). In the third, list the **judgments** or **decisions** made or reported in the lecture. And in the fourth, list the **attitudes** and **perspectives** involved.

Leave some space in each box and invite students to add to each list. Leave time towards the end of the lecture to review their suggestions.

Once students have become familiar with the fourfold schema above, you can prompt them to discern the structure of the discipline themselves by issuing sheets on which each of the four boxes are empty apart from their headings. Invite students to complete the boxes themselves. Since this is challenging, it may be helpful to use interim exercises – either divide the class into four groups, one for each box ('I'd like this group to list all the skills, methods, or techniques that we encounter') or leave only one box blank each time.

15 Problems

In **Problem centred and syndicate groups** (see **39**) it is suggested that students are presented with specific problems to tackle.

When giving students problems, you have a choice. You can either just tell them what the problem is or give it to them in written form, as a handout.

The handout has several advantages:

a   You are more likely to present the problem in an unambiguous form.

b   You are less likely to disadvantage non-native speakers and students with certain disabilities.

c   You are able to set more elaborate, demanding and interesting problems, requiring more skills of selection, analysis and synthesis of the students (e.g. case studies, simulations, data to be interpreted).

d   You can give additional supporting material at the same time, such as references to useful sources.

e   You can give an indication of the procedure which the students could follow in solving the problem. If the problem is complex, you can present it in stages, laid out in sequence.

f   If they have a handout, students can check back that they have remembered the problem correctly.

g   The piece of paper serves as a tangible focus for the students while they are working on the problem.

16 Questions

Lectures are often built around questions rather than conclusions or information: 'Is Britain capitalist?', or 'Would Impressionism have developed without the influence of Japanese art?'

But students will often overlook or ignore these questions because they feel safer with certainties and information. They need to be encouraged to see what the central questions are and to work with them. There are several ways in which this can be done.

The course content can be presented in the form of questions rather than topic labels. This may have the added advantage that students will begin to consider the answers to the questions beforehand.

The questions posed in a particular lecture and the subsidiary questions arising from them can be presented in a lecture handout. This will provide the direction and framework within which students can structure their notes during the lecture and evaluate new information when doing their follow-up reading and thinking. Such handouts can be very effective study guides.

Topics to be discussed in **Buzz groups** (see 38) or in subsequent seminars may also be best presented in the form of questions. Listing these questions on a handout ensures that all the students will undertake the same task. The more complex the questions and the more numerous the subsidiary questions, the more necessary these question handouts will be.

17 Uncompleted handouts

Conventional note-taking may be criticised for giving students too much to do in order to have the time to make sense of what is being said. However, full handouts which contain most of the key points of a lecture are open to the opposite criticism that they leave the students so little to do that they may find it hard to maintain their attention. Furthermore, the most useful notes after the event are personalised ones: those with unique elements of special personal significance to the note-taker. Notes prepared by others can be 'dead' and encourage little active negotiation of ideas.

An excellent compromise is to provide handouts with gaps in them for students to fill in, providing sufficient framework and details to remove a burden from students, and sufficient omissions to keep them active and give them a chance to personalise the notes. Examples of ways to leave gaps:

a   Include labelled axes of graphs, but leave the plotting to the student.

b   Include diagrams but leave the labelling to the student.

c   Include a table of data, but omit certain crucial figures.

d   List points: 1...
　　　　　　　　　2...
　　　　　　　　　3...
　　　　　　　　　4... for students to fill in.

e   Include a heading and leave half a dozen lines for the student to write in conventional notes.

f   Include partially completed calculations.

18 Article

Reading can be an effective learning activity during a lecture (see **42 Reading**). But while it may be reasonable to expect all students to possess and bring a particular text book, much of the source material for your lecture may come from journals. Undergraduates' unfamiliarity with the journal form and their inexperience in reading and 'gutting' articles quickly can make it rather unlikely that students will follow up the references one gives for articles. This is one of the traditional arguments made to justify lecturing: that it is the only practical way of making the content of journal articles accessible. But there is much to be said for working with journal material during the lecture, to increase student familiarity with such material and their motivation to use journals independently.

Before using a journal article that your library subscribes to, check the terms of its licence agreement. For example, inserting PDFs of articles directly into your institution's learning platform may be a breach of copyright. In many instances, it is possible to hyperlink to specific journal articles. Linking methods may vary between providers. Also, it is important to check links from time to time as they may not be stable.

Selecting key sections of an article – abstracts, the introduction, discussion and conclusion – can provide all you may require. This selection of key sections can also teach students how to get the main points from an article without having to read it all.

Once students have some familiarity with journals in this way, you might ask them to find a particular article and bring it to the following lecture. In the lecture, time can be devoted to reading, and discussing the article in **Buzz groups** (see **38**) or through **Pyramids** (see **40**) rather than lecturing about it. Those students who have failed to obtain their own copy will gain little from this section of the lecture. They are more likely to make sure they follow instructions next time. With such a penalty for failing to obtain a copy, the original instructions must obviously be clearly flagged (see 2).

Some lectures involve relatively brief reference to a whole series of experiments reported in the literature. A handout containing the articles in which these experiments were reported can both serve as an excellent aide-memoire and guide further study. As with handouts containing only the relevant sections of an article, an abstracts handout can lead students into using a literature source they might otherwise not use.

19 Reading guide

One of the functions of lectures is to prepare students to be able to read around the subject to better effect (see **1 Briefing**, example c). However, students' notes don't always contain the crucial information needed to read effectively: exact references, page numbers, comments about authors, warnings about inadequacies or theoretical biases and so on. A handout can be provided which is written to give a guide to reading, to be kept on hand whilst reading and whilst selecting books and articles to be read. A one-minute verbal gloss on such a handout can save 10 minutes of lecture time and provide much more adequate reference information than students' own notes are likely to.

Such reading guides can usefully be quite extensive, giving commentaries on books, suggesting alternatives, suggesting an order in which to read selected passages, and so on. The more specific is the information you provide, the more likely it is that students will actually read what you want them to. Reading guides are different from **References** (see **32**) in that while references enable you to find material, reading guides help you to read it effectively.

Chapter 4

Structuring and summarising content

20 Structuring — 53

21 Objectives — 55

22 Advance organiser — 57

23 Displaying the structure — 59

24 Progressive structuring — 61

25 Repetition — 63

26 Simultaneous messages — 65

27 'The three most important things…' — 67

20 Structuring

Almost all lectures have at least an implicit structure. Items are sequenced in a particular way for good reasons, and sections are related to each other in logical ways. A great deal of thought may have gone into the structure of the arguments and presentation. Or the structure may have been taken for granted and seen as being inherent in the subject matter. Either way the structure is very important. But it is the structure which students often have most difficulty in perceiving, and their notes often reveal only an undifferentiated linear sequence of content. If you can identify the key structuring elements of your lecture and give this information to your students, you can be very helpful to them.

Types of structure include:

a   lists;

b   classification hierarchies (e.g. 1, 1.1, 1.2; 2, 2.1, 2.1.1, 2.1.2; 3 etc.);

c   problem-centred lectures (e.g. a central problem, three possible solutions, and eight items of evidence to be accounted for or explained);

d   chaining (e.g. logical sequences built up progressively: 1, 2, 3; (1, 2 and 3) together; 4, 5, 6; (1, 2, 3, 4, 5 and 6 together); 7, 8 etc.) (See also **25 Repetition**);

e   comparison (e.g. comparing key features of two or three methods);

f   pattern. Patterns (also known as 'organic notes') represent the way an individual perceives knowledge in an area. Patterns start in the middle of a page and move outwards along lines of association or logical relation. Organic notes such as mind maps and spider diagrams are excellent for portraying how concepts cluster together and interrelate.[1]

g networks. Networks are more formalised patterns and are designed to show complex interrelations between factors. The example below illustrates the interrelated factors involved in designing project work.

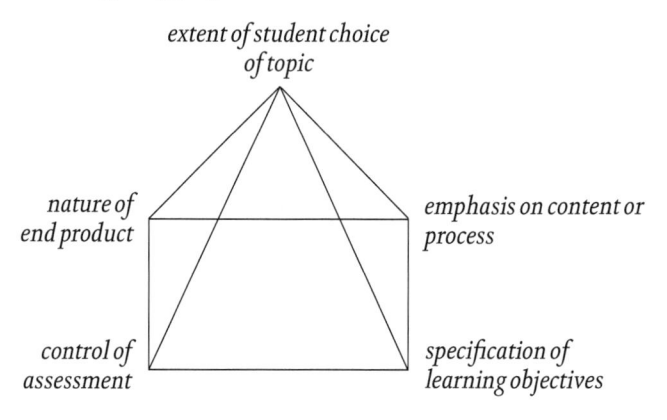

```
              extent of student choice
                    of topic
                       /\
                      /  \
        nature of    /    \    emphasis on content or
        end product /_____\   process
                   |\      /|
                   | \    / |
        control of |  \  /  |  specification of
        assessment |___\/___|  learning objectives
```

h logical dichotomies or matrices, e.g.

Forms of economies

	Capitalist	Socialist
Western countries		
Third World countries		

It is vital that lectures are not just structured, but also that the structure is perceived and understood by your students. (See **25 Displaying the structure, 24 Progressive structuring**.)

For fuller information please see:
Bligh, D., *What's the Use of Lectures?* Intellect Books, 1998.

Reference
1 Buzan, T., *Use Your Head*, BBC Active, 2006.

21 Objectives

Telling the students about the subject matter you intend to cover in a lecture, or even displaying the structure of that subject matter (see 23) may still not indicate to them what they should actually get out of the lecture. One effective way of doing this is to specify what you would expect students to be able to *do* at the end of the lecture. Specifying what students should *know about* or *understand* will not enable them to be clear whether they have actually achieved your objective. What would count as knowing about something?

Specifying objectives in terms of behaviour which you could observe makes it much easier to judge success. Once specified, such objectives can perform the function of structuring the lecture which is then geared around the achievement of these clear objectives. They can provide the basis of tasks for buzz, or problem centred groups to work on (see 38 and 39) and make the formulation of test questions easy (see 50–52).

Whole books have been written on how to write such objectives, but the basic formula is, 'At the end of this lecture you should be able to . . .' Use the following active verbs to describe the nature of the desired behaviour.

If you want your   . . . use one or more of these verbs
students to:

Know: state, define, list, name, write, recall, recognise, label, reproduce.

Understand: identify, justify, select, indicate, illustrate, represent, formulate, explain, contrast, classify.

Apply:	predict, demonstrate, instruct, compute, use, perform.
Analyse:	analyse, identify, differentiate, separate, compare, contrast, solve.
Synthesise:	combine, summarise, restate, argue, discuss, organise, derive, relate, generalise, conclude.
Evaluate:	judge, evaluate, determine, support, defend, attack, criticise, select.

Some educational objectives are not very amenable to formulation in this way, and when you attempt to write them you may find yourself writing rather a lot in the first category above, concerned with recall rather than understanding. The different types of lecture described in **Briefing** (see 1) clearly have quite different objectives, some of which are harder to draw up in this form than others.

If you find yourself writing objectives using verbs such as 'solve', 'apply' and 'evaluate', you may realise that passive note-taking is not an ideal way for students to go about achieving such objectives. The suggestions in this book under the heading of **Active learning during lectures** (37–47) are concerned with those sorts of activity which are more likely to achieve such higher-order objectives.

22 Advance organiser

The principal function of the advance organiser is to bridge the gap between what the learners already know and what they need to know if they are successfully to learn the task in hand.

When new material is introduced to students it is more likely to be understood and retained by them if it can be successfully 'anchored' to some previous knowledge. Then the previous knowledge serves to prepare the way for the new and makes it easier to learn.

If there is no readily available pre-knowledge for the new to attach itself to, then learning can be made more effective if some other basis is offered by the teacher.

Ausubel[1] gives a full description of 'anchoring' devices all of which have the characteristic that they are much more general than the new material which will follow.

For example, an introductory lecture on the Darwinian theory of evolution could start with the students discussing the idea of 'the survival of the fittest' or answering the question 'Where are the dinosaurs?'. A lecture on the history of the American Civil War could start with a brief extract from the film of *Gone with the Wind*, which offers a view of what life was like in the Southern States at the time of the Civil War. This would serve as the basis for the academic treatment of political and military history which would follow.

Another example of this method is given in **Drama** (see **44**) where a staged event is used to focus the minds of law students on the problems arising from the variety of conflicting statements from witnesses.

Reference
1 Ausubel, D. P., *Educational Psychology: A Cognitive View*, Holt, Rinehart & Winston, 1968.

23 Displaying the structure

There can be quite a gap between having a clear structure to your lecture and students' recognising that structure and being able to use it to help them understand and learn the subject matter. You can help to bridge this gap by using various devices to portray the structure to students. This portrayal may differ in form from the way you have written your own notes; what has helped you to organise the material into a lecture may not help students to perceive this organisation.

Diagrams and visual presentations often work better than spoken or written prose in portraying structure. Most of the structuring devices described in **Structuring** (see 20), though not patterned notes, can be used effectively to display structure and **Progressive structuring** (see 24) is often helpful for displaying structure.

It can be helpful to display a slide showing the lecture's structure at the start of the lecture. Instead of a brief 'Today we are going to be looking at . . .' it may be worth briefly running through the key elements of the entire structure so that students know what to expect and how one section will be linked to the next. Such a display can have quite an impact on the quality of students' notes.

Referring back to the overall structure by displaying it at intervals can reinforce this effect (see **24 Progressive structuring** and **25 Repetition**).

Displaying the structure at the end of the lecture can act as a learning check for students and help them to improve their notes.

24 Progressive structuring

Complex structures can be conveyed very effectively by presenting them in stages, progressively building up the whole structure as you explain its components. Instead of displaying the whole structure at the outset (see 23) you can use PowerPoint to display the structure as it develops. Typical uses are to build up a structured list, or matrix structure, or to progressively write elements into a bare framework.

Such progressive structuring is valuable when:

a   the structure is rather complex to take in all at once;

b   the way the structure develops and the way its components are related need to be shown;

c   changes over time (in historical developments, the elaboration of a theory, the development of a machine, etc.) need to be displayed;

d   uncovering new and unexpected information adds to the dramatic impact of the explanation.

However, progressive structuring can be overused. It is easy to be tempted to devise PowerPoint presentations using progressive structuring to try to enliven boring material by introducing an element of drama and suspense. Your students are unlikely to appreciate progressive structuring devices unless they genuinely aid understanding.

25 Repetition

Simply saying the same thing over and over probably doesn't have much of an impact on subsequent memory, especially over longer periods. But nevertheless encountering ideas and headings more than once in a lecture can be helpful. Repetition can be especially helpful if used in conjunction with structuring moves you make. At each stage, instead of saying, 'The next thing is (d) . . .' and diving in, you can repeat what has been covered so far: 'So now we've looked at (a), (b) and (c), and we can now go on to (d)'. You can go one step further than this and repeat the main elements of each section: 'In (a) we saw that . . ., in (b) we saw that . . ., in (c) we have just seen that . . ., and now we can move on to (d)'. Linked with the use of a slide which you use to display the structure so far, this form of repetition can really drum the points home (see **24 Progressive structuring**). This building up and rehearsal of the content of a lecture as it develops can help to link chains of ideas together and can work well when the lecture is structured as a story, investigation, or other logical sequence.

The example offered on the next page is from an Open University course on systems management. Every one of the 16 course units has this diagram on its back cover, illustrating the relationship of the units to each other and to the main themes of the course. The repeated use of this diagram hammers home the course's structure.

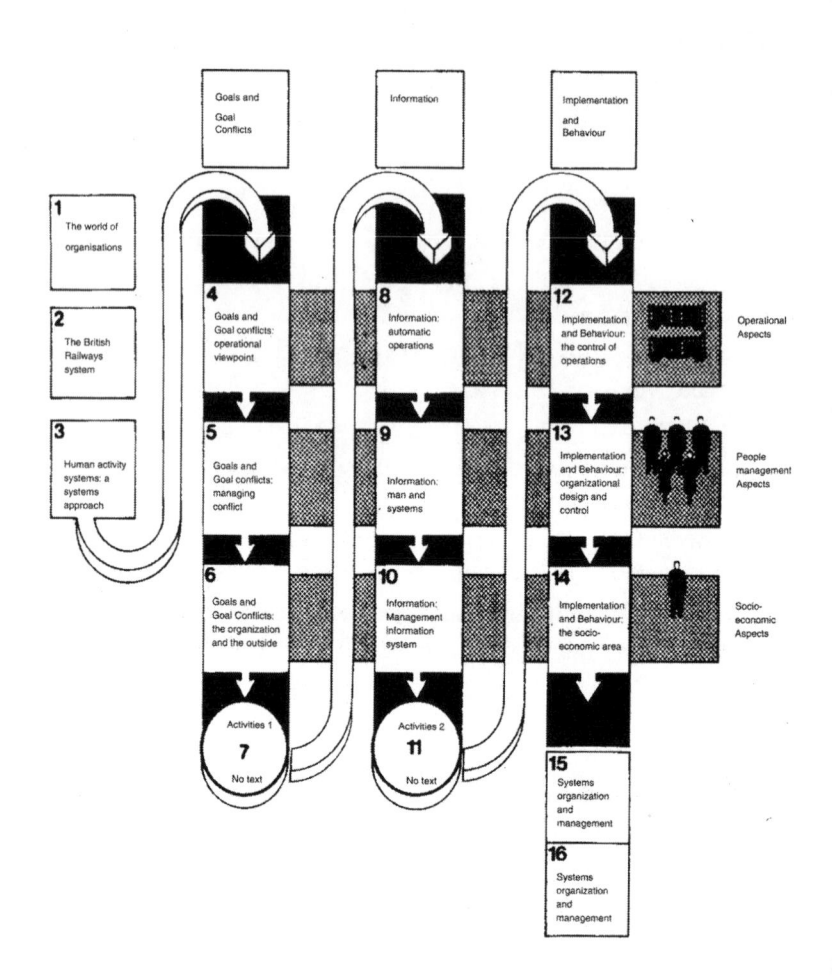

Repetition

26 Simultaneous messages

There is often a need to maintain a constant reference to one bit of information or idea while examining another. You may want to keep the original question posed by the lecture in front of students while you examine alternative answers. You may want to keep a complex outline of the logical structure of the lecture displayed while you are working through the structure, so that students can always see where you are.

In such circumstances it can be effective to use two separate audio-visual aids simultaneously: for example, using PowerPoint to display the fixed message while using the board or document camera to present detailed information relating to what you are currently explaining. We have used two visual aids simultaneously:

a   to present a graph and some data which need explaining on one, while presenting alternative explanations on the other;

b   to present category definitions on one while presenting examples for students to practise on the other;

c   to keep a list of points covered so far (see **24 Progressive structuring**) in front of students while exploring each point in more detail on the other;

d   to present information which would be too cramped and difficult to read on a single slide, and too difficult to make sense of if displayed sequentially.

Most of the applications we have encountered provide students with either an aide-memoire or a simple structure through which a complex idea or image can be conceptualised and learned.

27 The three most important things...

Even when clear structuring devices have been used at the start and throughout a lecture there may still be a need for a special form of summarising or highlighting at the end. Structures may represent the logical relationships between the elements of a lecture and emphasise the way these elements have been built up into the whole, but they may still not contain the overall message of the lecture. The whole is often considerably more than the sum of the parts and higher level, more abstract, theoretical or methodological issues may provide the overarching framework within which the lecture is located (see **31 Theme lectures**). The most important points in a lecture may not be contained in any particular sub-element and may not be identifiable in the clearest of structures.

Say, for example, you used a slide to portray the structure of a lecture on bat measurement. The structure is made up of a 3 × 3 matrix containing three methods along one axis and their description, advantages and disadvantages along the other axis. But the most important points about this lecture might be neither about specific methods, nor characteristic advantages and disadvantages, but rather about choosing a method to suit a particular type of bat, or even, more generally, about the context dependency of the choice of methods of measurement. It could be valuable to students for you to summarise such points by concluding, 'The three most important things about all this information on bat measurement are:

a   Different measurement methods suit different bats;

b   There are different kinds of error involved with different methods;

   c   The extent of these errors depends on the matching of methods to bats'.

If brief enough, such a statement could be displayed on a slide or included in a handout. This simple statement, 'The three most important things . . .', can be helpful as it rises above the sometimes overwhelming detail of lectures, and highlights those things that students would do well to remember, even if they forget practically everything else. Of course it could be two, four or five things, depending on the subject matter. One is too few: it is then too easy to elaborate on this one point so that its character and distinctiveness are lost to the students. More than five may become just another unmemorable list. The examination of students' notes (see **12 Looking at students' notes**) would reveal whether your summaries are being registered by students.

Chapter 5

Linking lectures

28 Last week, next week	71
29 Preparation activities, follow-up activities	73
30 Spot the links	77
31 Theme lectures	79
32 References	81

28 Last week, next week

While individual lectures may have their own separate identity and deal with a relatively discrete topic, they are usually placed where they are for special reasons. A lecture will follow the preceding one and precede the next because of the structure of the subject matter itself or because you want to stress particular relationships and juxtapositions of ideas. It can be important to share your reasons for ordering your lectures. Students often fail to perceive relationships between topics and deal with lecture topics as if they were completely free-standing. Also it is through the building of new knowledge onto old that the development of understanding takes place. Making explicit the links between last week and this week can give students handles with which to hold on to key organising ideas, and remind them of structures onto which this week's ideas can be grafted. Requesting students to review last week's notes for three minutes at the start of the lecture, giving a one-minute verbal summary of last week, or displaying the slide with which last week's lecture was concluded, can all help to make these links. Forward linking to the following week can be useful to enable preparatory work to be done before the next lecture, and enable students to start trying out the mental connections which will need to be made. Also, when next week's lecture is introduced at its start, the ideas will not be completely new to students and they will be able to start operating on what are already partly familiar lines, using partly familiar language. Setting a test on last week's lecture at the start of the lecture can work well to achieve backward linking, and setting a test on work which has been undertaken in preparation can achieve forward linking (see **50 Start with a test**).

It is common for teachers to underestimate students' difficulties in making connections. Whilst the teacher may spend her week on perhaps half a dozen main topic areas, the students may be faced with twenty, all new to them and all to be experienced in compartmentalised one-hour slots. A brief mention by the teacher of links is likely to pass students by completely. Such brief mentions are seldom evident in students' notes, however important they may be (see **12 Looking at students' notes**). When you deliberately draw attention to last week and next week you may need to flag explicitly what you are doing and stress its importance (see **2 Flagging**).

29 Preparation activities, follow-up activities

Lectures are seldom the only teaching and learning activity on a course. But the linking between lectures and other elements is often left entirely to students. For example, a reading list may be handed out after a lecture, but with no guidance as to what aspects to concentrate on, or why, and with no subsequent use made of any reading which might be undertaken. Similarly tutorials are often intended to provide a forum in which issues from the previous lecture can be discussed. But no mechanism is provided to bring such issues forward in a coherent and usable way, or to prepare students more thoroughly for such tutorials. Similarly courses and lectures are often designed on the assumption that students have specific prerequisite knowledge, perhaps gained on an earlier course or in an earlier part of the same course. But during the lecture in which such prerequisite knowledge is required it is rare for any action to be taken to revise or test this knowledge.

There are various ways of achieving fuller and more reliable integration, and most of them involve setting students very specific tasks to do either before or after a lecture.

In preparation it is possible to bring to the fore students' relevant or prerequisite knowledge by:

a   simply stating what assumptions will be made about student knowledge at next week's lecture;

b   designing brief exercises (e.g. reading a section of a text or answering a problem) the achievement of which will demonstrate possession of the prerequisite knowledge;

c   handing out a brief self-test, and asking students to make sure they can complete it correctly before the next lecture;

d   warning students of a pre-test to be administered at the start of the next lecture, to count for assessment purposes;

e   suggesting specific references which will be used in the following lecture in a way which assumes everyone has read them;

f   announcing that the following lecture will start with a buzz group or syndicate group activity to discuss a particular problem.

Follow-up activities can be generated at the end of the lecture, by:

a   leaving gaps in lecture handouts which can only be filled in by subsequent independent work or reading (see **17 Uncompleted handouts**);

b   asking specific questions or setting specific problems which will subsequently be discussed (perhaps in tutorials);

c   setting very specific reading tasks. Listing 23 texts may result in less reading than itemising 5 carefully chosen pages;

d   setting a post-test to be undertaken before the next lecture;

e   setting a specific task in preparation for the tutorial, e.g. 'Write down *three* questions you want answers to. You'll be expected to ask these in the tutorials';

f   displaying an exam question from a previous year on the topic of the lecture. This should demonstrate that the lecture provides an inadequate basis for answering the exam question and should also indicate what further work needs to be done;

g   identifying those aspects of the lecture which will be considered prerequisite knowledge for the next. Students are not always good at identifying what they can afford to leave blurred and half-learned and what must be mastered immediately if problems of understanding later sections of the course are not to build up. This last suggestion illustrates how the follow-up activity for one lecture can become the preparation activity for the next.

30 Spot the links

You may be careful in each of your lectures to explain how the lecture you are about to give connects to other lectures – especially the preceding and succeeding ones in the same series – and indeed to the course as a whole. Though this is a helpful, commendable practice, it does have one disadvantage, namely that it delivers intellection on a plate – rather than arouse curiosity and prompt discovery.

For a change, announce that you are going to refuse to elucidate the connections between the lecture and the rest of the course. Instead, issue students with a challenge – to find as many links as they can between your lecture and others. Explain that you will allow time at the end for students to make public the connections they have found.

The connections that students volunteer can sometimes be narrow in range – perhaps limited to topic. It may be helpful, therefore, to provide a list of tags to use. For example:

a   'topic' – the topic repeats, overlaps, or resembles that of other lectures;

b   'theme' – a main idea, whether or not expressed explicitly, recurs between lectures (offer a token prize for the best *implicit* theme);

c   'extension' – the lecture adds to or develops the picture or argument of previous lectures;

d   'analogy' – a pattern of ideas resembles a pattern in another lecture;

e   'perspective' – the lecture borrows a perspective used in another lecture;

f   'tension' – there is a contrast, difference, opposition, or dissonance between one lecture and another.

31 Theme lectures

The relationships between a lecture and other course elements, and between one lecture and another, are often mentioned in passing, or as a brief introduction or conclusion. However, such relationships may be the most important aspects of the course, and at the same time the most difficult for students to appreciate. Students' notes from lectures very often reveal their preoccupation with minutiae and factual detail at the expense of broad themes. In part this may simply reflect the lack of prominence given to broad themes by the teacher. It may be worth deliberately separating out these broad themes and giving a separate explanation of them (see **33 Mini-lecture**), perhaps accompanied by a student activity (e.g. **38 Buzz groups**). Such theme lectures may only be necessary every few weeks and may form the lecture element of **Lecture tutorials** (see **37**). The role of theme lectures may also be performed by **Theme summaries** (see **13**) as well as by course guides.

32 References

References form an important part of many lectures. Teachers often expect students to follow up references and do further reading. Students who have incomplete notes but full references can make good the inadequacies of the notes.

You can help your students with their references in a variety of ways:

a   Always give full references, in the format approved by the library. Give the page numbers for passages which you quote in the lecture.

b   Say why each reference is being given, using a coding system if it makes things easier.

   A simple coding system

   R   = read this
   R (ch 3) = read chapter 3 of this book
   O   = read *one* of these books/articles
   I   = read this if you're particularly interested in this area
   D   = don't bother to read this unless you're really keen – I've given you the reference just for the record.

c   Set aside a part of the board or use a slide to build up or gradually reveal your list of references.

d   If you make a handout giving references and quotations, this will save time in the lecture and ensure that your students have an accurate record.

e   In a lecture where references are basic to the structure, as, for example, a lecture dealing with the comparative views of a number of authorities on a particular subject, the handout can be built around the references, with the titles of books or articles as subheadings, followed by quotations, and with gaps for students to add their own notes as the lecture proceeds (see **17 Uncompleted handouts**).

Chapter 6
Holding attention

33 Mini-lecture 85

34 Breaks 89

35 'Now look at me when I'm talking' 91

36 Ottoman railways 93

33 Mini-lecture

The duration of a lecture is frequently determined by the one-hour slot allocated to it rather than by educational principles. There is evidence that students' levels of arousal, levels of attention, subsequent memory for information and amount of notes taken – in fact, almost every sensible indicator of performance one can think of – deteriorate fairly rapidly from early on in a lecture, reaching a very low level after 20 minutes or so. What is learned after 20 minutes is likely to be learned at the expense of material in the first 20 minutes which is then forgotten.

Evidence such as this has led us to suggest that activities and breaks of various kinds should be introduced every so often in lectures so as to try to restore attention and performance to their original levels and allow more lecturing (see 34 and 37–47). But an alternative way of responding to the limits of students' ability to attend effectively for long periods is simply not to attempt to lecture for long periods. If relatively little is achieved after 20 minutes it seems sensible to stop and do something else. Once one has reconceptualised lectures as much shorter events, all sorts of possibilities open up:

a Instead of separating lectures from their associated practical sessions in different timetable slots, the lectures can be given at the start of the practical and the lecture slot abandoned.

b Instead of separating lectures from their associated tutorials the lecture slot can be used for a mini-lecture followed by 40 minutes of structured discussion (see 37 **Lecture tutorials**).

c Instead of separating lectures from follow-up reading, students can spend the remaining 40 minutes of the lecture slot either reading their text book or handout in class, or as part of a specified reading task in the library.

d   Instead of forlornly hoping that students will prepare properly for lectures, you can use the first 40 minutes of the lecture slot for specific preparation tasks (including reading) and only the last 20 for the mini-lecture.

e   Instead of expecting students to cope with an hour of mathematical theory, to be followed up at some later date by practice problems, you can follow a 20-minute mini-lecture on theory with 40 minutes of a problem class in which students can practise problems whilst the teacher is available.

f   Instead of finding yourself repeatedly giving prolonged off-the-cuff explanations in what are supposed to be interactive tutorial groups, you can deliberately prepare one or more mini-lectures. Such mini-lectures may need to be only 5 minutes long. Such carefully planned brief explanations may be especially memorable and effective for the way they stand out from their background whereas if they were buried between 40 and 45 minutes into a lecture they might be completely forgotten.

An obvious objection to the mini-lecture (as to many of the suggestions we make concerning the introduction of active learning tasks into lectures) is that one can only cover a third as much in a 20-minute mini-lecture as in a full lecture. Our reply is:

a   While a teacher may cover more material in an hour, it is pretty clear that students do not also cover more material, except in the sense of taking more notes.

b   If students need to be given notes over a broader area, handouts can be provided.

c   Probably only 40% or so more ground is covered in a 55-minute lecture than in a 20-minute mini-lecture.

d   What is crucial to learning is the relationship between the lecture and more active subsequent learning activities. Any short-term advantage a 55-minute lecture may have over a mini-lecture is likely to be lost if adequate rehearsal and consolidation of learning are not undertaken very soon afterwards. Such rehearsal is rare when lectures fill their timetable slot and are followed by other timetabled activities (see **11 Review**).

34 Breaks

Levels of attention and rates of learning fall off fairly rapidly during lectures. Passive attention, in particular, is prone to a sharp decline over even quite a short period. Evidence suggests that after about 20 minutes, students are taking in very little. Documentary makers assume that about four minutes is the limit one can expect an audience to pay attention to the same image or 'talking head', and usually change the image at very much shorter intervals than this.

It seems that levels of attention can be raised to close to their original high levels by a variety of changes of activity or mode of audience response. Indeed most of the suggestions in this book have, as one of their justifications, this ability to restore levels of attention and performance.

But it is not only active changes which have this power of recovery. Even passive breaks can serve the same function. Simply calling out 'Take five!' and suspending all demands on students for a few minutes can have a very beneficial effect on subsequent performance and more than make up for the loss of time. During prolonged sessions (such as in symposia where one 20-minute presentation is immediately followed by another, without pause for breath, for up to two hours) this use of breaks is absolutely vital. Breaks which allow uninhibited physical movement, social chat, noise, a change of seat or a breath of fresh air work better than quiet restrained breaks. Effective learners know how to make use of such breaks to recuperate. (See also **43 Quiet time** and the example in **2 Flagging**).

Even very short breaks of half a minute can be valuable. By and large, the longer uninterrupted work has been going on, the longer the break needs to be; the longer the total elapsed time since the start of the session, the more frequent breaks need to be. Such breaks can be very useful and relaxing to the teacher, too. You can catch your breath, have a look at your notes, and compose yourself before moving on to the next section of the lecture.

35 'Now look at me when I'm talking'

The usual behaviour of students in lectures is to listen to the teacher and write notes but rarely to look at the teacher. Sometimes in a lecture you want students to look at you because you are pointing out something on the whiteboard or demonstrating a practical skill or piece of equipment or, more subtly, because they can learn something from looking at your facial expression, hand movements, etc. If you want them to look at you, you will need to make a firm statement such as 'Now I'd like you to stop writing for a couple of minutes and just look at me while I show you what I mean'.

If you want to be successful in gaining students' attention in this way you may need to take account of how the students may regard the suggestion. They may be thinking, 'Unless I take notes while she talks then I'm going to miss this bit in my notes because she'll just rush on to the next thing after this demonstration'. So you may also need to say, 'I'll give you a couple of minutes to take notes on this after you've watched me'.

36 Ottoman railways

I once attended a lecture on the rise of the Ottoman empire. The speaker identified a number of factors that explained the rise of the empire. One factor he mentioned was the development of railways in the region.

A little later he returned to the point, reminding the audience that what he had said could not possibly have been true, since the rise of the Ottoman empire preceded the invention of the steam locomotive. He explained he had included the erroneous idea to test whether we were listening.

The benefit of this ploy is that it wakes up not only those students who aren't listening, but also those who are listening but not thinking. Students listen more carefully afterwards to ensure they don't fall for any further tricks.

Include an equivalent for Ottoman railways in your subject – just make sure nobody leaves the room between laying the bait and expositing it.

Chapter 7

Active learning during lectures

37 Lecture tutorials — 97
38 Buzz groups — 101
39 Problem centred and syndicate groups — 103
40 Pyramids — 105
41 Tiers — 109
42 Reading — 111
43 Quiet time — 113
44 Drama — 115
45 Students as teachers — 117
46 Using the audience — 119
47 Debate — 121

37 Lecture tutorials

Lectures and their associated tutorials are normally treated as quite different events. They are usually held in different kinds of room, with different sized groups, and are separated in time by perhaps a week or even more. There are also considerable differences in aims and processes. In lectures students are passive; in tutorials they are supposed to be active. Lectures present the basic background information; tutorials discuss wider implications, applications, and so on. This extreme separation can cause very real difficulties in linking tutorials effectively with lectures, and it is a common experience for students to arrive at a tutorial with an incomplete understanding of basics lectured on too long ago for ideas and questions to be forthcoming, and with a passive and unreflective attitude induced by lectures. Such tutorials often turn into lectures as soon as the teacher struggles to inject some life into them. But it is not this kind of lecture tutorial to which we are referring.

Instead it is possible to fulfil many of the functions of the tutorial during the lecture itself by using some of the suggestions proposed elsewhere in this book (see especially **38 Buzz groups**, **39 Problem centred and syndicate groups** and **40 Pyramids**). Lecture periods can be divided between lecture and tutorial time (see **33 Mini-lecture**). You may need to have two lecture periods in order to complete the same amount of lecturing (but see **Mini-lecture** for answers to arguments about the importance of 'covering the ground') but you will be able to scrap your tutorials. In large groups this can save a great deal of time. You may be worried about the opportunity for individual students to raise specific problems which require more prolonged personal attention than is possible in large lecture groups (though it is questionable whether such a facility exists in tutorial groups of more than four). If so, it can be provided through 'surgery' hours during which you are available in your office. The following analysis illustrates the potential savings in time:

- a *Conventional method*
  72 students
  1 lecture a week
  1 tutorial a week for each student in groups of 6
  Teacher hours = 1 (lecture) + 12 (tutorials) = 13 hours

- b *Lecture tutorial method*
  2 × lecture tutorials a week
  6 × surgery hours
  Teacher hours = 2 (lecture tutorials) + 6 (surgery) = 8 hours

(In addition, surgery hours are very unlikely to be fully booked up and the time can be used in other ways.)

Advantages of such a lecture tutorial system include:

- a Teachers can avoid the boredom of many repeated tutorials on the same topic.

- b Students often discuss better and more openly in teacher-less groups.

- c Teacher-less groups often lead to self-help groups.

- d As the tutorial element immediately follows, or is bracketed by, the lecture, students do not have time to forget or get confused before the tutorial.

- e As the lecture element is immediately followed by discussion or some practical individual or group activity, attention tends to be much higher and involve more active thinking and less passive listening.

37 *Lecture tutorials*

f Lecture tutorials are easy to run. 50-minute lectures can be quite taxing to prepare and present, and small group tutorials can be painfully difficult to keep alive.

g It is possible to arrange discussion in much smaller groups than tutorial groups (which may have to be large for economic reasons).

h Students do not have to undertake any one activity for too long at a time.

i The larger the size of the lecture group, the more economical the method is.

38 Buzz groups

Students' experience of lectures is often characterised by solitude, passivity and, after twenty minutes or so, somnolence. To change this experience to one of lively social activity requires something more than 'talk among yourselves', which usually results only in desultory and aimless chat.

A solution is to require students to form pairs, and to set a specific question or topic to be discussed for a minute or two, and to do this every fifteen minutes or so. Buzz groups are named after the noise created when such instructions are given. Groups larger than pairs may be less satisfactory: they may be physically difficult to arrange in lecture theatres (but see **41 Tiers**), and may take longer to discuss a point. They may also allow individuals to 'hide' and not to participate. Pairs can quickly tackle small tasks and everyone is more likely to participate.

The kinds of task which you can usefully set include the following:

a   review the preceding section of the lecture;

b   apply or test knowledge from the preceding section;

c   allow students to ask their own questions about the lecture;

d   prepare the way for the next section.

Simple closed questions with right/wrong answers will fail to provoke much discussion. Ambiguous, over-general and over-large questions will stall students. Successful questions and tasks are those which make immediate sense and engage interest but are not immediately answerable or soluble.

Two minutes of buzz can restore students' attention and motivation for the next fifteen minutes.

Problems which teachers can experience with buzz groups include:

a   the immediate buzz of noise which can seem alarming, as if all control has been lost and may be impossible to regain. Indeed it may take a little assertiveness to end a buzz period of activity;

b   the fear that students are chatting about last night's football game or are discussing the fact that your socks don't match. Touring around listening to students is only likely to inhibit them. Requiring a few pairs to report back may reassure you;

c   the fear that what students are saying may be incorrect. Again you can ask a few pairs to report back, or you can provide the answer or solution to the task so that they can correct their own mistakes;

d   repetition of the same type of buzz group activity (e.g. 'Share your notes with your neighbour') which may become boring. Try to build up a repertoire of varied buzz group activities.

Buzz groups can be distinguished from **Problem centred and syndicate groups** (see 39) because they are briefer, involve smaller tasks and smaller groups, and need not entail any reporting back or pooling of points.

39 Problem centred and syndicate groups

Students seldom learn what you are lecturing about while they are still in the lecture room. They may develop an immediate sense of familiarity and even of understanding, but this isn't likely to lead to longer term improvements in their ability to use their new knowledge without further application, practice, and so on. The most efficient time for applying a new idea is immediately. In mathematics and engineering it is common to design problem sheets for students to practise new techniques explained in the lecture. But this practice is often intended to take place online at some later date. In social science and the humanities it is quite rare to expect students to apply new ideas to a problem situation, still less to do this during the lecture in which the ideas were presented. Apart from the importance of immediate rehearsal and application of new ideas and methods, the other major reason for setting students problems during lectures is that they can gain from working with each other in groups and from seeing what alternative solutions others arrive at, so gaining immediate feedback.

Problem centred groups, or syndicate groups, are small groups of students (4–6 is ideal) who have been set the same problem to work on, simultaneously. On completing the problem, groups report back to the teacher in the hearing of the other groups. If an entire session is devoted to syndicate group work then the furniture can be arranged so that each group can clearly see the teacher, and blackboard or screen, without having to disturb their group. In a lecture the size of syndicate groups may be constrained by furniture. In tiered lecture theatres groups of four (with alternate pairs turning round) may be the limit (see **41 Tiers**).

The way Bligh[1] describes problem centred groups involves each group leaving a chair vacant to allow the teacher to join the group should the students request her help. In contrast **Buzz groups** (see **38**) and groups formed during **Pyramids** (see **40**) benefit from privacy and teachers may interfere if they join them.

Because problem centred groups are best used to tackle more substantial problems over a longer period of time, groups are more likely to welcome and benefit from help.

Reference
1 Bligh, D. A., *What's the Use of Lectures?* Intellect Books, 1998.

40 Pyramids

Pyramid or 'snowball' groups involve students first working alone, then in pairs, then in fours and so on. Normally after working in fours they return to some form of activity involving the pooling of the conclusions or solutions of the groups. The method was developed by Andrew Northedge[1] of the Open University for tutorial groups of mature students. But it has some special advantages if individual or small group work is to be used during lectures:

a   Setting individual students a task to do during a lecture may not work well if there is no clear demand on the student to produce an outcome. On the other hand, demanding that individuals report the outcome of their work in public in a large lecture class can be very unnerving: they are likely to focus their attention on avoiding being picked on to report, or if asked, on getting through the experience as painlessly as possible, rather than seriously attending to the task in an open and exploratory way. Suggesting that students take the outcome of their individual work to their neighbour involves just enough social obligation for them to get on with the task, without too much threat of humiliation if they don't get very far with it.

b   Using buzz groups may sometimes work only slowly because students may come to the 'buzz' without any ideas formed or anything much to say. They may cope with this embarrassing situation by starting to work on their own: by re-reading their notes for example. Once working on their own they may then never get going in discussion. If students are instead given even a very short period to work on their own to prepare some ideas beforehand, then they are much more likely to start a useful discussion straight away.

c   Syndicate groups of four to six may have difficulty in getting going from cold, especially if the lecture room furniture is unsuitable and they have previously been passively listening to a lecture. It is relatively easy to speak and get involved in a pair and once started it can then be much easier to get going in a larger group. One minute spent alone and three spent in a pair can save ten minutes at the start of a syndicate. Students need the time and opportunity to try out new ideas in safe surroundings before they are likely to risk sharing them in a larger group.

d   Going straight into syndicate groups also risks starting half way through a problem or prematurely closing down options, rather than starting from the beginning and considering alternatives before choosing one to pursue. Different instructions to students working on their own, and then in pairs, can ensure that the basic steps of problem solving have been worked through by the time a larger group grapples with the problem.

e   Individuals, and even pairs, may be quite reluctant to report the outcome of their work in public. But when students are asked to report on behalf of a group of four or eight, which has been formed through pyramids, they seem much more willing to do so. They speak more confidently and coherently than under other circumstances. This seems to be because they have already rehearsed some of the ideas before in smaller groups, will certainly have spoken already, and are likely to feel that they are not solely responsible for the ideas: 'These are not my own ideas, you understand, but those of my group!'

f   Students working alone may feel that their own solutions to problems or ideas are the only solutions and ideas, or at least that they have arrived at these ideas in the same way as everybody else. Similarly, groups often develop their own consensus and unified approach to a problem surprisingly quickly. Pyramids progressively confront students with ideas and assumptions different from their own and does not allow groups the comfortable complacency of immediate consensus.

g   Some tasks may be complex and difficult to tackle all in one go. Individuals may get stuck through lack of knowledge or ideas. Groups may be very poor at organising themselves so as to make use of their collective knowledge and ideas, and may progress rather slowly. Pyramids can make complex tasks more manageable, especially when each stage is accompanied by a progressively more complex and demanding task which builds on the achievement of the previous stage. To illustrate:

On your own
'OK, I have spent the last 20 minutes explaining about valuation methods. I want us to try applying this to a practical situation, the valuation of an office block. We are going to pyramid the problem I've displayed up here. So first, on your own, write down the important bits of information which you will need to use to do this valuation. Separate the useful stuff from the noise. You have two minutes.'

In pairs
'Now, in pairs, quickly check your lists of information to see if you agree. When you've done that, get going on doing the valuation. I'll give you 5 minutes. I don't expect you to have completed it in that time; just see how far you can get.'

In fours
'Right, you've had 5 minutes. Please form fours by combining two pairs. Explain to each other what you've done so far. Have you

gone about it the same way using the same method? I'm going to give you another 10 minutes to try and complete this valuation, but before you get going I'd like you to go through the methods I've explained today and agree between yourselves which method is most appropriate in this case. When 10 minutes are up I'll ask a couple of groups to go about this valuation.'

Plenary
'OK, 10 minutes are up. Now this group over here, can you just tell the others how you have tackled this one? How does that compare with that group? . . . And have any other groups gone about this differently?' etc.

The tasks need to be built up in this way because pyramids can be boring if the same task is used at each successive stage and students simply find themselves explaining the same thing over and over to different audiences.

Pyramids can be undertaken in a group of any size. We have used it in groups of more than 400, and with sub-groups reaching 16 before reporting back.

Having a rapporteur appointed within each group of four improves the quality of reporting back and saves time. The expectation that your own group might have to report back is quite important in maintaining a little tension and motivation. If you can ask every group at least one quick question when it comes to reporting back then this will keep them on their toes next time. A certain amount of time pressure can help induce a little urgency and pace to group work, though too rapid progress can trivialise tasks and produce superficial work and reporting back.

Reference
1 Northedge, A., 'Learning Through Discussion in the Open University', *Teaching at a Distance*, No 2., 1975.

41 Tiers

Lectures are often held in tiered lecture theatres where the seating is fixed. This may seem to work against flexibility. In fact, it is a very good situation in which to use **Buzz groups** (see 38). Students are already sitting very close to one another and can easily form groups without having to move: the students on rows 1, 3, 5, etc. turn round to face those on rows 2, 4, 6, etc.

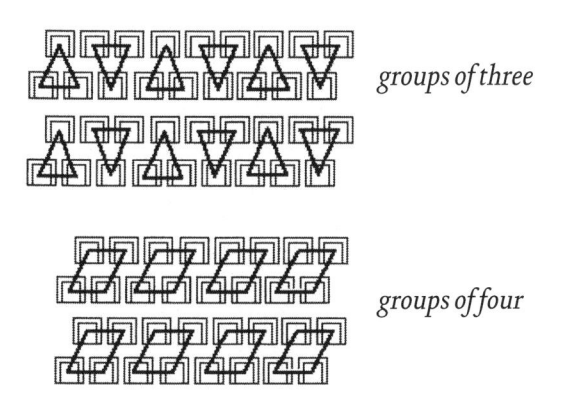

groups of three

groups of four

While it may be a bit chaotic the first time you ask students to form such groups in a tiered lecture theatre, they soon get used to forming groups quickly and quietly.

42 Reading

You can read several times faster than you can listen to someone reading out the same text. And the text you have read can then act as a perfect set of notes, whereas if you are trying to listen to a fast presentation you will have trouble taking notes at all. Reading is also more flexible than listening: you can go at your own pace over difficult or boring bits, re-read sections, stop and think or add comments without missing what comes next, and so on. If a good text exists, then reading it is far better than listening to a lecture. You need to have some fairly sound reason for wanting to lecture at all with such competition.

The choice between lecturing and asking students to read is not an all-or-nothing one. Frequently lectures are a combination of basics (found in textbooks) and elaborations, which are more or less personal, or combinations of original sources and commentaries. The basics and original sources might be better read, leaving your unique contribution to be made in lecturing on the elaborations and commentary. Such a division would also vary the students' learning task to good effect.

We have, on occasion, replaced entire lectures with a suitable text (even a specially written text!) and instructed the audience to read a section, discuss it in threes, ask us questions for clarification, and then continue to read the next section, and so on, working through the complete text. This takes about as long as it would take to read out the text without any discussion or questioning.

Despite teachers' sense of the importance and correctness of their own personal way of expressing ideas, students seldom have their perspective, very often perceive books to make a better job of it, and fail to appreciate the subtle differences which might have led the teachers to reject the text book and decide to lecture in the first place. Lecturing is perhaps best left for those occasions for which no suitable text can be found. Reading during lectures has the added advantage of ensuring that at least something is read by the students and that they are introduced to books or authors you would hope they would read further.

An objection to the reading of even good texts in class is that relevant information and key passages may be spread about a bit rather than neatly located in one place. But students should have the reading ability to overcome this problem, or if not they should be taught it. Instructions for such a situation might go something like this:

'You now have 15 minutes to find out what Eysenck has to say about the relationship between race and intelligence. You will find references to him are clearly marked in the index. Most of these are in Chapter 3, pages 75–92, and especially on pages 83–84. Make notes summarising Eysenck's views, and any problems with, or objections to, these views you can see. In 15 minutes' time you will have the chance to discuss these views and your criticisms of them in groups of three. I'll then give a brief summary of my own and some views of my own.'

43 Quiet time

Something missing from many teaching methods, and especially from lecturing, is time for private reflection. In a lecture students' thinking tends to be at the expense of hearing. It can be valuable to stop even at quite frequent intervals to allow a moment's thought, and deliberately to plan longer breaks every 10 to 15 minutes – perhaps only lasting a minute. A minute's silence seems quite a long time when in a lecture! At the end of a lecture a more prolonged quiet time may be useful.

To make quiet time work it is important to insist on silence, to avoid students chatting about the previous night's football match. Reflection can be difficult in a bustling atmosphere.

The drawback of quiet time is that students may have difficulty in reflecting without a specific task to guide their reflection (see **38 Buzz groups, 15 Problems, 11 Review**). Its advantage is that it leaves students free to pay attention to whatever concerns or interests them.

It can be tricky giving instructions for quiet time because the surest way to stop someone thinking is to say 'Think!' to them. Initially you may need to make suggestions such as 'Read the handout', 'Check through your notes', 'Summarise that last idea in you head' but when students are used to it you can just call, 'Quiet time! You've got a minute to yourself. Please don't talk' and leave it to them to decide what they do with it.

Quiet time can also give you a moment to pull yourself together, get your notes sorted out, and get the next part of the lecture clear in your head. This can make lecturing a much less stressful activity.

44 Drama

While a particular lecture may stand out for the teacher and particular ideas within that lecture may have special significance for the teacher, the students' perceptions are likely to be somewhat less discerning and more jaded. They may sometimes attend a dozen lectures in a week, a hundred in a term, over five hundred before they graduate. Many lectures may be attended in the same room, even viewed from the same seat. From such a perspective it seems that making key ideas notable and differentiating them from the vast mass of background can be a considerable problem.

One effective way of giving prominence to a key idea is to dramatise it. Rather than theorising about why dramatisation seems to work we will simply recount dramatisations we have experienced which have been memorable for us and hope these give you ideas.

In discussing the effects of very low temperatures on the properties of materials a teacher brought along an ordinary plastic football and bounced it while talking. She then placed the football in a container of liquid nitrogen while continuing her explanations. At the appropriate moment she retrieved the football from the container and bounced it on the floor. But instead of bouncing, it shattered into a thousand pieces with a loud bang. The unexpected noise, and the contrast, gave the demonstration a dramatic effect which made it quite unforgettable and aroused a lot of curiosity.

In a lecture on legal witness and the giving of evidence, several students rushed into the lecture room, created a disturbance and then left. The intervention had been planned by the teacher but was not expected by the audience. The audience was then asked to give verbal testimony as to what had happened, to illustrate various problems in the use of evidence from witnesses.

In a lecture on metre in poetry, the teacher played a drum in rhythm with the metre of the poetry she was reading out, in order to demonstrate the points she was making.

44 *Drama*

45 Students as teachers

In this book we describe a number of situations in which students work in pairs (see **6 Swop, 11 Review, 40 Pyramids**). A common feature of these situations is that in each case the student works on her own material, notes, ideas etc. with the assistance of her partner.

In some situations students might become more like teachers to their partners and work with them to explore areas of difficulty, differences of approach, and so on, as in the following examples:

a   If part of the lecture is being used to complete a calculation (see **17 Uncompleted handouts, example f**) students can help each other with areas of difficulty.

b   Where a student has answered some test questions incorrectly (see **50 Start with a test, 52 Spot test**) she may call upon her partner to explain her errors and how the correct answer is arrived at.

c   In a particularly difficult lecture pairs of students might describe their difficulties to each other and try to help each other.

In this delicate and potentially difficult situation, such exchanges of assistance can be made more acceptable and successful if you give your students these ground rules:

a   Don't criticise, laugh at, or in any way depreciate your partner for his or her ignorance or apparent stupidity. Be understanding and helpful.

b   Don't tell anyone else about your partner's problems. This is just between the two of you, in confidence.

c   You will not be asked to report on what you have discussed, either here in the lecture, or afterwards in the tutorials. If you want to raise your own problems in the tutorials that's up to you.

45 *Students as teachers*

46 Using the audience

In the theatre various devices are used to engage the audience more directly and actively, rather than leaving them as passive onlookers. Beyond direct appeals and rhetorical questioning is a range of methods which may require physical action or verbal interaction with the actors. Similarly in lectures it is possible to engage the audience in the process of the lecture instead of leaving them as passive observers of it, in order to enhance interest, understanding or retention.

We use this device most clearly when teaching drama, when we assign parts to members of the audience who then enact a scene from a play being studied.

In subject areas such as social work which are concerned with human interaction, members of the audience can be assigned roles in brief role plays to demonstrate techniques or pose problems. There is evidence that students observing role play or simulation involving their peers also gain significant benefit. For example, showing health science students video clips of simulated diagnostic discussions between pairs of students or students and tutor has been used to good effect in developing conceptual language and confidence in the area of clinical reasoning.

In the sciences, 'metaphorical' role play can help students to visualize abstract concepts such as respiration or photosynthesis. Students portray specific parts of a process and interact with each other (for example, immunology students acting as cells of the immune response and using props to simulate cell activity). Such role play can be particularly effective at reinforcing lecture material. As in the previous example, research has suggested that observers learn as much from the process (e.g. in test scores) as participants.

When complex calculations need to be done on the blackboard, parts of the calculation can be assigned to different individuals or different sections of the room. Or one half of the room can be asked to use one method for the calculation while the other half uses a second method, in a race to see which works better. Using a member of the audience, or a syndicate group, to come to the front to explain the outcome of the problem they have just been working on, can also engage the audience.

46 *Using the audience*

47 Debate

A problem with lectures in subject areas where there is controversy or a number of different schools of thought is that a single teacher may present a somewhat one-dimensional view of the subject. While it is obviously possible to attempt to present all sides of an argument, it is difficult to avoid either making one's own view look very much the strongest, or else lapsing into grey objectivity and a comprehensive relativism.

It can be more engaging for the audience if alternative viewpoints are put by two individuals who feel free to put their own case uninhibitedly while strongly criticising the other's case. Elaborate formats with panels of participants, and a chairperson, are not necessary. We suggest the following format:

a   two teachers, each prepared to argue a case and criticise the other's;

b   a debate title. You don't need anything too dramatic. There is plenty of scope in such ordinary questions as: 'Is D. H. Lawrence a sexist writer?' 'Box girder bridges: success or failure?' 'Is "Reaganomics" economics?';

c   an uninterrupted presentation of the two cases for not longer than 20 minutes each and preferably only 10 minutes;

d   each presentation to be followed by two or three 'difficult' questions asked by the opposing teacher;

e   questions from the floor after the opponents have finished. Prepared questions can work better than spontaneous ones, if students are in a position to prepare these in advance;

f   a show of hands vote on the issue of the debate.

It is possible to engage the audience more actively by forming buzz or syndicate groups to discuss the cases, to prepare questions, or to make their own contributing statements. Debates can of course be held by the students themselves, but this is moving away from the lecture format and is not considered here.

Chapter 8

Checking on learning

48 The instant questionnaire 125

49 The three most important things…
for students 129

50 Start with a test 131

51 Finish with a test 133

52 Spot test 135

53 'Are there any questions?' 137

48 The instant questionnaire

An important characteristic of questionnaires is that they gauge opinion rather than measure things more directly. A test, for example, can measure the extent to which students actually know certain things or can do certain things, whereas a questionnaire can indicate their opinion as to whether they know or can do these things. Provided you trust their judgement (and if you are using questionnaires as feedback rather than as assessment there is no reason why you should not) then questionnaires offer a very quick way of getting feedback compared with tests which can be time-consuming to design and check through.

Using the example of a lecture on bat measurement (see 27) one might pose the following questionnaire items to gain feedback on the lecture:

1 I could list four ways of measuring a bat.

2 I could choose the best method for a given bat.

3 I don't understand why you use Slow methods.

4 I can explain three sources of error.

5 I need practice at measuring bats.

6 ... etc. ...

Students would respond to each of these statements by indicating their level of understanding according to a three-point scale:

    1 = Yes
    2 = Don't know/not sure
    3 = No

If your AV resources include a student response system you might prepare your questionnaire in advance as part of your slide presentation. However, a truly 'instant' questionnaire is prepared in the lecture itself, and can be 'low tech', for example, written on the board and containing just a small number of statements such as the five listed above. This can be done during a **Quiet time** (see **43**) or a **Buzz group** (see **38**), for example, so you can match your statements very closely to your current concerns about how that particular lecture has gone. Students respond by taking a sheet of their own paper and writing down the numbers of the statements and next to them writing 1, 2, or 3 (the three-point rating scale), e.g.:

    1   2
    2   1
    3   2
    4   1
    5   3

The students hand their sheets in at the end of the lecture as they leave, and you collate the data. If you like, you can also add the open-ended questions: 'What do you not understand fully?' and 'What aspects of this lecture would you like to spend more time on?' to pick up any other information which your chosen statements failed to cover.

The usual rules apply to formulating good statements:

a   Avoid ambiguous statements.

b   Avoid double statements such as 'I could list the advantages *and* disadvantages of Slow methods'.

c   Mix positive and negative statements and those which are likely to elicit 'yes' and 'no' to avoid biasing responses.

48   *The instant questionnaire*

d   Avoid exaggerated statements which encourage the student to make a misleading reponse: 'I can remember absolutely nothing whatsoever about Slow methods'.

e   Use statements about behaviour such as 'I could list...', 'I could explain...' which produce responses which are easier to interpret than statements about thoughts such as 'I understand...', 'I know...'

The use of the instant questionnaire has been proposed here only for gaining feedback on student learning of the content of the lecture. We do not consider evaluation of the process of lectures in this book.

49 The three most important things... for students

Earlier in this book (see item 27), this method was suggested as a means of summarising the lecture at its close in order to highlight its most important features. This same device can be used to check on student learning.

You could say, 'Right, that's the end of this week's lecture, but before you go I'd like to check whether I've got my main points across. I'd like you all to write down the three most important things about this lecture: those three things that, if you forgot everything else, would capture the essence of the lecture for you. You have two minutes'.

While students are doing this you write down what you think are the three most important things on a visual without letting students see your points. When the two minutes are up you display and briefly explain your three points and why they are the most important. You then ask for a show of hands: 'Who, honestly, has written down all three of these points? Who has written down two? Who one? Who none? What other points did people consider important?'

If this seems too threatening to students you can:

a   emphasise that what is on trial is your own competence as a teacher rather than their competence as learners;

b   ask for their points before revealing your own;

c   collect up students' written statements to read in private;

d   emphasise the scope that exists for alternative perspectives, different conclusions, etc.

This exercise can be very salutary.

50 Start with a test

Starting a lecture with a brief test can serve a variety of very useful functions:

a   Tests of material dealt with some while ago can serve to review and rehearse that material so that it is established more firmly in your students' memories.

b   When preparation for the lecture is important, giving advance warning of a test on the prepared material will make it more likely that preparation is undertaken thoroughly, and will highlight weaknesses in preparation.

c   Where the structure of the subject matter is hierarchical and your lecture requires previous knowledge, a test can provide you with feedback on whether students have this knowledge.

d   Students coming straight from a lecture on a different subject may need a minute or two to re-orient themselves to your subject and focus on those ideas which they will need in order to make sense of your lecture. A demanding task such as undertaking a test can function very effectively, and quickly, to help students to get their ideas together on your subject.

e   In selecting questions you can highlight links between this lecture and previous topics you have examined.

f   By asking questions which students will not be able to answer you can highlight what they do not yet know, and so indicate what this lecture has to offer.

Items (e) and (f) can be used together as a way of making clear what the lecture will be about.

Such tests can be set by displaying a slide, or by using handouts (see **16 Questions**) and students can be asked to work on these questions alone or in small groups (see **38 Buzz** and **39 Problem centred and syndicate groups**). If you want to save time, then use multiple choice questions rather than open-ended questions and use a student response system if available.

51 Finish with a test

Finishing with a brief test is a good way to round off a lecture and provide students with feedback on how much they have understood and learned in the lecture. Such tests also have other uses:

a   In answering test questions students are reviewing the lecture and going over the ground again, reinforcing their learning.

b   Test questions which cannot be answered demonstrate to students where follow-up work needs to be undertaken.

c   Tests can be set which are intended to be tackled during a subsequent tutorial, or which are intended to be tackled during the last few minutes of the lecture but discussed during a subsequent tutorial. This provides continuity with the tutorial.

d   The test can be handed out at the start of the lecture with the instruction: 'In the last ten minutes I'll ask you to answer these test questions. So keep them in mind while I'm lecturing and think about how what I say can be used to answer them'. This can help to establish the objectives of the lecture and to focus students' attention on what matters.

Tests can be set in handouts (see **16 Questions**) or on slides. Students can tackle them alone, or in small groups (see **38 Buzz** and **39 Problem centred and syndicate groups**). Answers can be provided verbally, on slides, online, by asking individuals to check with their neighbour, in subsequent tutorials, or at the start of the next lecture. A test can be readministered at the start of the next lecture as a way of linking the lectures (see **50 Start with a test**).

Although test material can be provided online for students to complete afterwards, many students prefer to complete tests during the lecture, appreciating the benefits of immediate reinforcement of learning, the chance to discuss and check understanding and avoiding the danger of not making time to follow up online material.

52 Spot test

Students who are accustomed to being given notice of tests may relax and stop paying attention on days when they know they are not going to be tested. So you may prefer to take your students by surprise occasionally.

Spot tests are simply tests which are sprung on students without warning. They may be of the same form as those described earlier (see 50 and 51). Spot tests may be very brief and quite frequent and may consist of, for example, one or two questions asked at the end of each section of a lecture or a small problem for the students to work on alone immediately after you have worked through one on the board, and so on.

The advantages of spot tests are that students need to pay attention at all times in case they are tested, and that a test which follows some brief exposition serves both to rehearse the material and highlight what is important about it.

53 'Are there any questions?'

The ubiquitous 'Are there any questions?' at the end of a lecture is so routinely ineffective that it has come to mean 'That's all for today'. During a lecture it doesn't work very much better. There are some good reasons for this:

a   Students may be too busy writing notes on what has just been said to formulate a question.

b   Dictation or fast presentation requiring full note-taking does not encourage thinking of any kind, let alone questioning.

c   Only brief silences are normally tolerated during lectures, and sensible questions may take a few moments to formulate.

d   An unspoken ground rule may be operating to the effect that getting through to the end of the lecture quickly is the primary goal. Questions may result in the teacher having to rush later on or even miss out the last section of the lecture altogether. This may cause more problems to students than the failure to have their questions answered, and so they collude with the teacher to avoid interrupting the presentation.

e   Even when a student has managed to formulate a question, she may need an opportunity to 'try it out' (to check that it doesn't seem silly) before she is prepared to ask it in public.

f   Students who ask questions run the risk of being considered stupid, attention seekers or geeks.

As a result it can be unusual for invitations to ask questions to be taken up. The larger, more formal and impersonal the setting, the less likely it is that students will ask questions. To get round these problems the teacher may need to:

a give students time in which to formulate questions;

b give students the chance to check out that their questions are not silly before asking them in public;

c ask everyone to formulate questions so as to avoid the stigma attached to the questioner.

You could say: 'Now I'd like to give you the chance to ask me questions about what I have just explained. You have half a minute in which to write down the question you'd really like to have answered, or a query you would like to raise. OK, I'm going to go along the third row back asking each person in turn to read out their question. So... What is your question?'

Or, 'Could you please turn to your neighbour and raise any question you have at this stage. Try and answer each other's questions. If you can't, write the question down. In two minutes I am going to ask a couple of pairs what their outstanding questions are'.

53 *'Are there any questions?'*